RARE BIRDS: VOICES OF HOLLOWAY PRISON

Natalie Scott is a poet and educator from the North East of England. She is the author of *Berth: Voices of the Titanic* (Bradshaw Books, 2012), and two pamphlets: *Brushed* (Mudfog, 2009) and *Frayed* (Indigo Dreams, 2016). Both *Berth* and *Rare Birds* received Arts Council England funding to be adapted for the theatre: the latter was workshopped with an award-winning team of West End actors and composers, and showcased at the Soho Theatre in London. Natalie shares her working time between the north and south, as a freelance writer for community projects and Creative Writing Lecturer at Arts University Bournemouth. She has a cat called Fizban (the Fabulous) and once folded Sir Peter Ustinov's pyjamas. Find her on Twitter @NatalieAnnScott.

Rare Birds

Voices of Holloway Prison

Natalie Scott

Valley Press

First published in 2020 by Valley Press
Woodend, The Crescent, Scarborough, YO11 2PW
www.valleypressuk.com

ISBN 978-1-912436-25-5
Cat. no. VP0145

A CIP record for this book is available from the British Library.

Cover and text design by Jamie McGarry.

Printed and bound in Great Britain by
Imprint Digital, Upton Pyne, Exeter.

Contents

Acknowledgements

Thanks are due to the editors and organisers of the following in which versions of these poems first appeared: *Algebra of Owls, Amaryllis, Dream Catcher, i am not a silent poet, Ofi Magazine, Orbis, Poetry Shed, Riggwelter, The Writers' Café Magazine, Whirlagust, York Literary Review*.

'Colonel Barker' was longlisted in the *Live Canon* Poetry Competition 2018, and published in their anthology of the top 50 (out of 2500) poems. 'Katie Gliddon' received Highly Commended in the *Yaffle Prize*, 2019. 'Nameless Prostitute' was longlisted by *Magma* for the 'work' edition, 2019. 'Muriel Matters', 'Katie Gliddon' and 'Emily Wilding Davison' were commissioned by Apples and Snakes as a performance podcast *Assembly – Women's Suffrage*.

The writing of this collection was greatly assisted by a 'Research and Development' grant from Arts Council England.

I am grateful for the support of Dr Debbie Challis and Anna Towlson at The Women's Library and Jeremy Smith at The London Metropolitan Archives whose archived material inspired some of the poems in this collection. Thanks also to Dr Rachel Bennett at Warwick University for sharing research on women in prisons and maternal health.

A special thank you to Glyn Maxwell, who guided me through the collection's early development on the page. Also to Gillian Clarke and Carol Ann Duffy who offered support and feedback at the Tŷ Newydd Writing Centre Poetry Masterclass.

The workshop and performance of Rare Birds at Soho Theatre in London (May 2019) was supported by a 'Grants for the Arts' award from Arts Council England. I am especially grateful to Simon Greiff (Deviser and Director) and Michael Webborn (Musical Director and Composer), plus composers: Rebecca Applin, Pippa Cleary, Jess Green, Kate Marlais, Grant Olding, George Stiles, Tim Sutton, Sarah Travis, Caroline Wigmore and Laurence Mark Wythe; cast: Martyn Ellis, Danielle Hope, Rachel John, Wendi Peters, Oliver Savile, Simon Thomas; and filming crew: Oliver Boito and Chris Walker.

Heartfelt thanks to the Tees Women Poets (TWP) Dianne Casey*, Jo Colley, Ann Cuthbert*, Julie Easley, Ellen Griffiths, Gail Henderson,

Kirsten Luckins, Susie McComb, Janet Philo* and Judi Sutherland, who first performed poems from this collection; to The Deadline Poets for all the encouragement in getting my poetry submissions out there; and to the Black Light Engine Room, Word Club and Beehive Poets for being supportive listeners as the poems developed.

Thanks also to the following for their kind comments and support along the way: Marie Alvarado*, Francis Annett*, Jade April*, Natalie Baron, Adrian Beard, Heidi Beck*, Kath Bingham, Pete Bingham, Christopher Braithwaite*, Carole Bromley, Yvonne Broome*, Caroline Chadwick*, Becky Cherriman, Leah Christensen*, Di Coffey, Mark Connors, Garry Craig, Andy Croft, Ruth Cull, Caitlin Davies, Sally Dixon, Julie Donaldson, Peter Dudas*, Carl James Dunning, Jennifer Essex, Kate Evans, Emma Falk, Michael Farren, Sarah Faulkner, Victoria Field, Bob Fischer, Alex Fleming*, Eric Foster*, Kate Fox, Tony Gadd, Harry Gallagher, Raine Geoghegan, Mary Norton Gilone, Michael Greavy, Annabel Grey*, Oz Hardwick, Graham Hartill, Barbara Hickson, Rod Huddleston*, Tracey Iceton*, Claire Jennings, Debs Kelland*, Helen Kirk, Gill Lambert, Liz Leek*, Harry Man, Carmen Marcus, Gábor Maszlag, Kim McDermottroe*, Mel McEvoy, p.a morbid, Marie Naughton, Robert Nichols*, Emily Owen, Mike Pratt, John and Sheila Pattison*, Claire Price, Michael Ray*, Adrian Salmon, Dorothy Scott*, Nick Scott, Tony Scott*, Clare Shaw, Anthony Slack*, Denise Sparrowhawk*, Emma Storr, Diane Taylor, Brian Thurlbeck*, Ken Vipond*, Rob Walton, Marianne Wheelaghan and Joe Williams.

And finally, loving thanks to my most stalwart supporters, my family and dearest friends (some already mentioned… you all know who you are!) xxx

also kindly supported the project via the GoFundMe crowdfunding campaign

Introduction to Holloway Prison – The First 100 Years

The City Prison at Holloway was conceived as an idea in 1842. Designed by architect James Bunstone Bunning, its first stones were laid on a plot of land originally intended as a burial site. The foundation stone was placed by the Lord Mayor, Sir James Duke on September 26th 1849, with its inscription threatening 'terror to evil-doers'. Holloway looked more like a gothic castle in appearance, with its imposing battlements and turrets. On October 6th 1852 the prison opened its gates to women, men and children over the age of eight; it had capacity for 400 inmates.

Originally intended as a House of Correction, Holloway had all the latest gadgetry, and prisoners actively contributed to its running through hard labour. Females partook in needlework, knitting, picked oakum or worked in the laundry. Males worked the treadwheel which pumped water into the building from a well. But discipline was strictly in place. The prison day lasted from 5:30am till 8:55pm with gas lights being turned off at 9pm sharp.

Prisoners were accommodated according to division, determined by the courts and dependent on whether their crimes were criminal or non-criminal. Second-division inmates' cells measured seven feet wide by thirteen feet deep and prisoners slept on a hammock suspended just above the floor. Cell doors had a spy-hole and a trap so that warders could check on inmates and admit food and drink. Some prisoners of the first division had comfortably furnished private apartments and could order in meals from the Holloway Castle tavern. They were not required to participate in hard labour and had their cells cleaned by a warden or a lower division prisoner. Additional wings were added to the building from the 1880s, so that Holloway could accommodate nearly 1000 prisoners.

On August 16th 1902, Holloway became a prison for women and girls only. An execution shed was constructed on site and the first inmates to be executed for their crimes were Amelia Sach and Annie Walters. Nevertheless, most of the women in Holloway were serving time for petty crimes such as drunkenness and prostitution; many of them were recidivists (repeat offenders). They spent 16 hours per day locked in their cells. A new team of female warders was employed, though they didn't receive the same pay as their male counterparts. Holloway's governor, chaplain and doctor at this time were all male.

In 1903 the WSPU was formed by Emmeline and Christabel Pankhurst. A more militant suffrage organisation with a motto of 'Deeds Not Words', it encouraged the acts of violence and protest which led to suffragettes being interned at Holloway from 1907, in the D and DX wings. At this time prisoners were classified as first, second or third division. Most suffragettes entered Holloway in the latter two categories, but in 1910, under Rule 243A, they were moved to First Division and could have some of the special privileges awarded to this class; this was still commonly connected to the wealth and social status of the individual. Many endured forcible feeding during their time in Holloway; a procedure akin to torture, which took its toll on the physical and mental health of inmates. This eventually led to the introduction of the Temporary Discharge for Ill Health, or Cat and Mouse Act, of 1913. With the outbreak of the First World War in 1914, all suffrage prisoners were released and the militant campaign came to an end. Many of the prisoners admitted to Holloway during the war period were declared enemies of the state according to the Defence of the Realm Act.

Holloway underwent a positive change in the 1920s, due to the influence of the first female inspector of prisons, Dr Mary Gordon and first female deputy governor Mary Size. Inmates had access to more exercise, better ventilation and the infamous arrowed uniforms were abolished. Prisoners were encouraged to see their families and could earn a wage doing prison work. The prison ethos became one of reform rather than punishment, with mutual respect and kindness encouraged between staff and inmates. At this time Holloway had about 100 staff divided into 'nursing' and 'discipline'. Young offenders were no longer given jail sentences but were sent to Borstals with an aim of corrective education and reform rather than punishment.

This positive change for Holloway continued into the 1930s, with prisoners being active in either work or education throughout the day. Recidivism was less common during this period. Women were allowed access to health and beauty products and had mirrors installed in their cells, an idea supported by Governor John Morton. The building even underwent its own makeover, with the dreary shades of brown and orange being replaced with pastel colours. Punishment cells became activity rooms and the condemned cell and execution shed, which supposedly housed the ghost of Edith Thompson, were demolished.

With the outbreak of the Second World War, two thirds of the prison population (those serving sentences of three months and less) were released and the remainder were transferred to Aylesbury. Cells soon began to fill with inmates who had received no trial and were convicted of no crime, yet were declared 'enemy aliens', some of whom were held under Defence Regulation 18B. Others were interned as conscientious objectors. The population rose to over 800 inmates. Many of these women were separated from their children. Being understaffed and overcrowded, Holloway's standards of cleanliness and hygiene deteriorated during this period.

In May 1945, Dr Charity Taylor became the first female governor of Holloway Prison. During this time Holloway housed many of the Borstal girls who could not be accommodated at Aylesbury. Many of these young women had been victims of physical or sexual abuse but were still recorded as having a criminal background. Two more women were executed at Holloway in the time leading up to 1955 – Styllou Christofi and Ruth Ellis – with the latter being the last woman to be hanged in the UK by Executioner Albert Pierrepoint. He declared that executions 'solved nothing', and retired from service the year following her death.

'Two women looked out from prison bars,
One saw fog and the other stars.'

Louisa Garrett Anderson
from Holloway Prison
Tuesday 26th March, 1912

'What does the past tell us?
In and of itself, it tells us nothing.
We have to be listening first,
before it will say a word;
and even so, listening means
telling, and then retelling.'

Margaret Atwood
'In Search of Alias Grace'
The American Historical Review, 1998

'And I think about what I have just seen
– a bird stripped of its fine feathers
in the cage of a condemned cell.'

Elizabeth Neilsen
Mother of Ruth Ellis
Sunday Dispatch, 3rd July, 1955

for Mum and Dad

and

in memoriam
Fred Bingham
(1945-2018)

Foundation Stone

Inscription on the stone laid by Lord Mayor,
Sir James Duke, September 26th, 1849
– viewed two ways

MAY GOD PRESERVE THE CITY OF LONDON
AND MAKE THIS PLACE A TERROR TO EVIL-DOERS

PLACE

PRESERVE

THE CITY

OF EVIL AND

THIS MAY MAKE

LONDON A

TERROR TO

GOD

DOERS

Major Arthur Griffiths

Inspector of Prisons 1878-1896 and later a novelist,
under the pseudonym of Alfred Aylmer

Ladies and Gentlemen, roll up, roll up!
Come see the petrifying parade
of prisoners, pacing round the garden
where the sunflowers grow tall.

Dressed as they entered, observe
their attire ... such a wide and wondrous
variety, but *please note* that they are
all the same in their evil tendencies.

Come see the petrifying parade of prisoners.

See first the "crooked gentry", the men
who thought they could have their cake:
bounders and cads in frayed frock-coats,
slack top hats and drab, sagging gaiters.

In degenerate suits, we have the artisan,
the coster, the street-loafer, the tattooed
seafarer, and, ah yes, the unmistakable
foreigner ... Ladies, *don't* get too close!

Come see the petrifying parade of prisoners.

Unmistakable roughs, fierce beasts,
swindlers, imposters, blackmailers, cheats
to the good of society. Gentlemen, note
how they hang their heads in shame.

Now, a treat ... the criminal women:
sad sisters whose outfits don't match.
See Ladies, how this one wears both
satin skirt *and* coarse shawl. Quite so!

Come see the petrifying parade of prisoners.

Such a wide and wondrous variety,
I'm sure you'll agree, but *mark my words*
they are the *same* in their evil tendencies.
So, please Sirs, I advise you ... *don't touch.*

Ladies and Gentlemen, roll up, roll up! ...

Emma Mary Bird

For Want of Sureties: Prisoner No. 1, 1852

30.	Going on a hundred.
5'.	And a half. Don't forget the half inch.
Sallow.	Yesterday I only ate scraps.
Dark brown.	Like the lovely flowing Thames.
Grey.	You're not looking hard enough.
Slender.	Pick me up and I'll snap.
None.	No job I'd tell you about, anyway.
Assault.	He touched me first.
6 months.	Could be worse.

New Arrivals

Inspected by the Governor, 1864

Flannigan, Sir. Fourteen,
and fourteen days I'll be here.
Pickpocket and a very bad boy.
My face says I'm proud of it, yes.

Brown, Sir. Seventeen,
and no mother or father, no,
but I want to go to sea. Six weeks
I'll be here for you to watch over me.

Gould, Sir, Gould, nineteen
and like a son to you. You taught me
a trade so I'd be set but I stole
I stole again and now I'm back.

Collins, Sir. Twenty-one,
and thirty-third time inside.
Not my fault, no. Drink, drink
always sends me to the clink.

Morris, Sir. Twenty-five,
And yes, I insulted my Maker.
I lied about having fits, I lied
to get out of hard labour.

Prisoner No. 6151

Guilty of begging – sentenced to 7 days with Hard Labour, 1865

My name? My name is
Lydia. Lydia Clements.
Do you need it spellin'?
Want me to spell it, dear?
My weight? Put me
on that thing and tell me
my weight.

I know 'ow 'eavy I feel
and it's not even as near
as light as I look. 'Ave I
confused you, dear? Why
not note my weight in
loaves of bread, or bags of
sugar, or cakes of soap?

So, I am eighty bags of sugar.
Sounds a lot for these bones,
and I'm far from sweet, dear.
Seven days in 'ere and I'll
soon be clean, clothed, fed.
I might put on a few bags.
Wouldn't that be grand, dear?

My age? My age is, well, I
think it is eighty, eighty-nine,
yes. Yes, eight and nine, dear.
One year shy of ninety. And
my name is Lydia Clements.
Do you need it spellin'?
Want me to spell it, dear?

Voices through the Walls

going on and on and on and on and on

you may now kiss the bride

pick me up and I'll snap

thought-clogged mind

I see only walls

let me plump your pillows

I am the antonym

they leave me cold

enjoy the fantasy

I wait for his cry

there was a young woman named Mollie

I suffer for my art

like someone else's skin

we melt in the sun

locked me up good

I can handle a month

in here I may dry up

I remain, remain, remain

do I even say these words

happily ever after

I move into the light

going on and on and on and on and on

John Weatherhead

Second Governor of City Prison, Holloway, 1863

By the twitching of my sideburns
something wicked this way comes.

I have an instinct for criminals.
I sense when there's rot in the room.
A festering wound that won't heal
no matter the layers of bandage.
You look concerned. Don't be.
You have nothing to fear. *I see.*
(Anyway, I would have sensed it.)

We take care of our prisoners here.

Sensitivity is required for this job.
I know when someone is lying
about being ill, mad or having fits.
Rest assured I take care of it.
Six weeks of cold-water drenching
and they soon find they recover.
(It's no use having fits in Holloway.)

We take care of our prisoners here.

Like this wretch in front of you.
Said he couldn't control his fits.
Just a ploy to avoid the treadwheel.
Nothing wrong but plain idleness.
So I designed this straightjacket
now he's as still as Scrooge's grave.
We take care of our prisoners here.

By the twitching of my sideburns
something wicked this way comes.

Selina Salter

One of the first 'lunatics', 1867

They said I been a bad girl
so they locked me up good.

I ruined the books, tore out
some leaves. Tried to eat

a psalm. I cried and cried,
so they moved me out

then locked me up good.
I pulled down a shelf and

snapped a table leg,
missed the chamber pot.

They sent me home to Pa
but he couldn't sort me out

so they locked me up good.
I ripped a nightgown

while it was still on. I wouldn't
pick oakum for the pain and I

cried, I cried, I cried. So
they sent me away on a ship.

But I found my way back
and they locked me up good;

this time, not rattling in a box
but strapped to a bed.

Dietary Requirements for Females

From the 'Regulations for the Government of the City Prison at Holloway', 1860

Class II

Convicted Prisoners for any term exceeding seven days
and not exceeding twenty-one days. (LESS SERIOUS CRIMES)

Breakfast	Oatmeal gruel*, 1 pint. Bread, 6 oz.
Dinner	Bread 6 oz.
Supper	Oatmeal gruel, 1 pint. Bread 6 oz.

Prisoners of this class, employed at hard labour,
to have in addition 1 pint of soup** per week.

Class V

Convicted Prisoners employed at hard labour, for terms
exceeding four months. (MORE SERIOUS CRIMES)

Sunday, Tuesday, Thursday and Saturday:

Breakfast	Oatmeal gruel, 1 pint. Bread, 6 oz.
Dinner	Cooked meat, without bone, 3 oz.
	Potatoes, 1 lb. Bread, 6 oz.

Monday, Wednesday and Friday:

Breakfast	Cocoa, 1 pint. Made of flaked cocoa, or cocoa nibs, sweetened with molasses or sugar. Bread, 6 oz.
Dinner	Soup, 1 pint. Potatoes, 1 lb. Bread, 6 oz.
Supper	Oatmeal gruel, 1 pint. Bread, 6 oz.

* The gruel to contain 2 oz. of oatmeal per pint. On alternate days to be sweetened with molasses or sugar or seasoned with salt.

** The soup to contain, per pint, 3 oz. of cooked meat, without bone, 3 oz. of potatoes, 1 oz. of barley, rice, or oatmeal, and 1 oz. of onions or leeks, with pepper and salt.

Boys under 14 years of age to be placed on the same diet as females.

Cutpurse

1866

Look into my eyes
and tell me you don't
feel your darkest desires
swelling inside of you.

It only takes an instant.

I'm the Dick Turpin
of purse-cutters. I belong
to the cleverest class of thief;
a charming plunderer.

I wear my hair a little longer
than other men, a carmine
kiss waits on my lips, my eyes
are delicately lined with soot.

It only takes an instant.

There is so much more
under this cape but you won't
get to taste the goods, though
you imagine the consequences

of trying. I have a penchant
for *La Parisienne*. Les femmes
magnifique, with their fashion
for double pockets.

It only takes an instant.

It's all in the eyes;
these respectable women
are not accustomed
to being looked at this way.

Their bodies soften, until
it's only their corsets holding
them up. Then, with a gentle
'Pardon, Madame', I'm in.

It only takes an instant.

A swift slice detaches
the chatelaine, then I
hold the keys to the castle,
(and the lace handkerchief).

The Governor says he'll take me
by the hand, assist me.
He's also fallen for my charms
and in my palm he floats.

It only takes an instant.

So, if you please, enjoy the fantasy
for a moment. Let me turn
my hand to you, for it is true
I can turn my hand to anything.

Prisoner whilst in Cell

1855

three shelves like a
tiered
wedding
cake
cornered in the cell

blankets: pair of, pillow, pair of sheets, rug,
      horse-hair mattress, hammock,

spoon: wooden, plate, gruel tin,
      salt-cellar: wooden

combs: two, hymn-book, prayer-book,
      floor-scrubber, Bible, brush,

not one item out of place
except me, the misplaced bride
    watching
          their
              shadows
                    drag

Mr Barre

Schoolmaster, 1859

Learning is like electricity;
that static crack
of chalk on slate; that
flash of a moment
when one of them
gets it right.
Ideas fizz
in a lightning
of electrons; the charged
components of the circuit.
I teach numbers
to silk-lipped blackmailers
and to fraudsters
apt at arithmetic,
I teach
the beauty and rhythm
of words.
It is all about
improvement.
Education is key. Show
an interest in the individual
and he might just
behave.

The Two Griffin Statues

Above interior gate of prison, carved in Caen stone by John Hemmings, 1852

In my talons
I clasp the
stone-cold
representative
of your lost
liberty. Its
real form will
haunt your
nights in
hard echoes.
Look up at
me; revere;
repent; be
truly petrified.

    i see only rough-
hewn versions
of them as they
pass through
    all face from
this height
    blackened
and blanched
    like moons
tilting dizzily
towards me
    i want to help
but my fate is as
carved as theirs

Pickpocket

10 years old, 1855

A right dab 'and I was. Come
by omnibus with a load of others,
off and through the main gate,
past them ugly birds with their
greedy beaks lookin' down on us.
I 'ad to get booked in first
like some 'otel. Said me name,
age, faith; they wrote me sentence,
'ad me scrubbed (I 'ad vermin
you see). I'd managed to grab
a nice "piece" the day afore
and it were still in me pocket.
I watched the screw 'andle it
'is eyes full of it, sparklin'.
There weren't a set of clothes
small enough so I 'ad to wear
a big set, all trussed up
at the top, middle and bottom.
It weren't so bad – I got
an 'ot meal in me belly. Lessons
were good too. Mr Barre said
me letters was comin' on.
I got me name out on slate
just afore me time were up.
A right mess, but 'e said
it showed promise. And it
were *mine*. I'd never seen
me name spelled out like that.
Chalky white lines on black.
Felt like I'd *finally* arrived.

W T Stead

Editor of Pall Mall Gazette and campaigner for equality.
Guilty of abduction – sentenced to two months, 1885

Our laws state that a girl of thirteen
is at the age of consent, and yet she is
not old enough to give witness in court.
My crime? Caring too much. I wanted
exposure, so I bought a girl and sold her.
Her parents accepted a slim price
and the brothel madam paid a slim price.
Deal done. Evidence acquired.

Our current laws don't protect those
who make it their calling to pull back
the stained bed-covers of crime.
I was charged with abduction because
her parents could not fathom
how they could have done such a thing,
so pretended they hadn't. Deny
all knowledge. Safest bet.

Our laws gave me time in Holloway. Not
so much a punishment as a treat. A
pleasant holiday in an enchanted castle. I
had a gas stove and kettle. Hot meals from
the tavern. I was in a state of journalistic
leisure with my books, paper, ideas. I
composed articles behind bars and passed
them for print. Luxury of time and space.

Our current laws allow such a waste
of resources. And the little girl is back with
parents who may sell her again if they
so choose because her voice is too young
to have a say, though her body is old enough
to have a child of her own. So she may
give birth at fourteen. And her life
will be over before it has begun.

Mary Ann Sutherland

Guilty of conspiracy to obtain money under false pretences
– sentenced to 5 years, 1887

Real name's Mary Ann
Catch me if you can!

Pious woman to start
Had such a sacred heart
Spiritual meetings
Strong tea and preachings
Charm was way off the chart

Real name's Mary Ann
Catch me if you can!

Next became Miss Bruce
Loved to cook the books
Purse full of cash
So made a dash
After adjusting my looks

Real name's Mary Ann
Catch me if you can!

Transformed into Kate Miller
As fraudster oh what a killer
Pure Scot and well-bred
To Australia I fled
Life is a page-turning thriller

Real name's Mary Ann
Catch me if you can!

Then Mrs Gordon Baillie
Crofters' friend twice daily
Collecting expenses
Under false pretences
Toasting them all at the ceilidh

Real name's Mary Ann
Catch me if you can!

Even convinced Willy Stead
The Gazette's cutting edge
Urged his readers
Poor old bleeders
To make a generous pledge

Real name's Mary Ann
Catch me if you can!

In here I'll bide my time
Reflect on my forty-nine crimes
Play little games
Making up names
For my next little pantomime

Real name's Mary Ann
Catch me if you can!

Rev. James Cohen

First Chaplain, until 1860

I am gladdened
that you have come to me,
for in my company
you will not be judged. You will
find acceptance and understanding.

Feel free to share
your misdemeanours
and I will not be shocked.
Neither will God, for He has
a timeless love for us all.

Look deeper into your faith
and doubts, reveal your pent-up
guilt of past indiscretions.
Let the names of those who helped you
fall heavy from your lips.

And you will find not
judgement and trial but rather
God's redemption as you are a part
of the body of Christ;
he will protect and guide you.

I am gladdened that you
have come to me, for in
my company you will not be judged.
You will find acceptance
and understanding.

*Chaplains were encouraged by authorities to elicit private information
from prisoners under the guise of religious and reformative discussion.*

The Order of the Administration of the Lord's Supper or Holy Communion

1869

And if any of those be an open and notorious
evil liver, or have done any wrong to his neighbours
by word or deed, so that the congregation be thereby
offended; the curate, having knowledge thereof,
shall call him and advertise him, that in any wise
he presume not to come to the Lord's Table,
until he hath openly declared himself
to have truly repented and amended
his former naughty life, that
the congregation may
thereby be satisfied,
which before
were offended;
and that he hath
recompensed
the parties, to
whom he hath
done wrong;
or at least
declare
himself
to be in full
purpose so to do,
as soon as he conveniently may.

Prisoner in Chapel

c.1860

I wasn't clever enough for classes
so I 'ad to write somethin' about chapel.
A – what did 'e call it? – a press...
...a pressis. Precise? I know he kept
sayin' it like I couldn't 'ear 'im.
Like just repeatin' it would
help me get its meanin'.

I thought it might be a kind of story.
So 'ere I am starin' at a clean page
wonderin' how to start.

Stories 'ave good 'uns and bad 'uns.
I know that much. An' a place. Here.

So us is huddled on pews – rows and
rows of 'em. An' them sit
arrow straight at the front.

Facing us. Staring. Judging us.
Are we the bad 'uns or them?

And the priest, well 'e had a mouth on 'im.
An' a voice like toothache. I could tell you
'ow many lines were on 'is face
but I couldn't for the life of me remember
precisely what 'e said.

Prisoners not deemed to be suitable for lessons
were asked to write a précis of the chapel service.

Henry Mayhew

*Journalist and social researcher, reporting on what
female prisoners wear and do, 1862 – reshaped*

In winter, three wincey petticoats
In summer, two wincey petticoats
Petticoats, petticoats, petticoats
Checked neckerchief in blue
Blue gown, printed handkerchief
Neckerchief, handkerchief, neckerchief
White linen cap, substantial shawl
Blue worsted stockings, pair of
Cap, cap, cap, shawl, stockings
Knitted by the female prisoners
Prisoners, prisoners, prisoners

Also occupied in employments:
Picking oakum, general cleaning,
Picking, picking, picking, cleaning
Nursing, needle-work, laundry-work
Nursing, nursing, work, work, work
Female prisoners in the laundry
Wash, fold and repair the clothes
Wash, wash, wash, fold, fold, repair
Of all inmates, even the males
But are allowed a pint of beer
Pint of beer, pint, beer, beer, beer

Prisoner at Exercise

1877

When there's no noise, my mind
sings to its own tune, to
a rhythm that matches
these rough-shod feet scuffing
forth as we pace the yard.
As we pace, pace the yard.

I stare down at them till
they no longer seem mine,
till I'm told 'Look ahead'
and I see only walls.
(Even if there is more,
I'm blind to it. So blind.)

My breath is a polluted mist
that clings between us;
I imagine the poor
wretch behind, walking through
it, and the one after
him, and him, and him and…

We file one after the other,
round and along and round
again, till the cold turns
us unnatural tones;
colours our mothers wouldn't
want us to be. To be.

And someone, somewhere up
there is listening close
to fifty pairs of feet
tramping the same old path
and wondering whether
we deserve this monotony.

Warder on Duty

Observing prisoners in the exercise yard, 1877

They walk whilst spaced three yards apart,
with skin of blue and red and white.
Shivering wastrels so void of heart,
they walk whilst spaced three yards apart.
In silence as the clouds glow dark;
a tricolore of baseness and vice.
They walk whilst spaced three yards apart,
with skin of blue and red and white.

May Caroline, Duchess of Sutherland

Guilty of contempt of court – sentenced to six weeks, 1893

A social climber, moi? I sell your papers, do I not?
Your creative juices flow, do they not, each time you

think of what I did? The next salacious headline dripping
from your lips. Does it not pay your wages? It's not my

fault he fell for me. I'm easy to love, am I not? It's not my
fault that a man far more tender and capable than

you granted me the power. (That's the only way women
can get it, you know.) I was made executor of the will.

Should I have disobeyed my beloved's last wishes?
The family jewels were left to me and they didn't like it.

It must have been a mistake. "Why would Father pin a
legacy onto a woman so far, far, far down the chain?"

Was I not the victim here? Yes, I did destroy the letter.
The law doesn't protect people skilled enough to

write things that may or may not be true. They are
always taken as fact when the time comes. Is this not

a miscarriage of justice? You would sell your soul
to know what it contained. A murderous plot or just

a string of obscenities? Either way you would be
satisfied. Does that not make you worse than I?

You have lust in your eyes for my suffering in this
dungeon, mixing with commoners. Imagine me,

with tears pricking my eyes, slipping out of his late wife's
underwear and donning a pair of knickers stained

from the last inmate. Well, dream on, red-faced boy...
I'm First Division! I have a veritable palace, with articles

specially selected: couch, curtains, mirrors, flowers.
Surrounded by dainty things. I dine courtesy of caterers.

Satisfy my healthy appetite thrice daily. I see whom I
want when I want. It seems unfair, does it not? So take
it up with the authorities! Or have you lost your

vigour for fighting now? A social climber. Let's see.
If you want to call me that, do. Because there is no

suitably fitting epithet for a woman who falls
in love with a man who fully deserves her, despite

their differences in station. But, do try to remember,
it's more difficult climbing a ladder wearing a dress.

Warder on Duty

Observing Oscar Wilde during his incarceration at Holloway for
one month whilst awaiting trial for Gross Indecency, 1895

The 'special cell' is my charge.
A more fitting room for big names
and even bigger money.
They bring their own chairs
and monogrammed paper.
But the key makes the same sound
in the lock as all the others.

From what the papers said
I expected a leering monster
who might try and steer me
towards his perverse ways.

Gross indecency was his charge.
It meant big things to me.
'Dirty things', my mother said.
He had 'an incurable disease'.
I wondered what would happen
if he touched me. Would I get it too?
I knew he had a famous imagination
but how far would it go?

He was allowed his own clothes
and the luxury of long hair.
When he sits in his armchair,
cross-legged, head rested on
one hand, his long fingers
propping the weight of his
purple-threaded thoughts,
to me he looks like a king.

He always speaks kindly
when I remind him of what he
can't do. He wants cigarettes, 'badly,
my dear boy' but takes 'no'
with a noble acceptance.

He endures the routine exercise pacing
round the yard in the rain, mute
and emotionless but returns looking
like he's solved the world's problems.

He says there are no seasons here.
His way of coping. Maybe if there
is no summer he cannot miss the sun.

Even when prison procedure strips
his privacy by lamplight and I watch
him undress then get into bed
like a child, he takes it all with a weary
elegance. Prison hasn't beaten him yet.

Later, through the spyhole
I see his pale, restless face, his mouth
shaping poetry, silvered by moonlight,
and I wonder if I *did* catch his 'disease'
whether it would be such a bad thing at all.

New Wardresses

Recruited, 1902

We were the fortunate few, whittled
down from a rough-cut huddle of hopefuls.
We thought we were the strongest women in England.

Our suitability determined by our physical state,
personal habits, character and conduct. They wanted
to make sure we were serious.

"Serious as sin," I said.
But they didn't find that funny.

We exchanged our children for heavy sets of keys
that swung from our hips. New blood
to nurture in these thick walls.

The 'grand tour' showed us the garden and the little
brick building: a lichen-free misfit within
the castle walls. Its slit windows just high enough

to conceal what went on inside.
When we asked if we could have a peek they told us
it wasn't a place for women.

Major Arthur Griffiths

1902

Misconduct, chronic and persistent, intensified by hysteria, these unsexed creatures respect no authority. At times the place is like a pandemonium.

Before we condemn these degraded specimens of the softer sex we should remember what they have suffered.

Nameless Prostitute

1903

Doing this job is a bit like riding
the merry-go-round
but it's them that keep feeding
coins to the man with his hand on the lever
None of us gets to choose our steeds
all painted the same with a line of teeth
Or the speed
of the ride

We go up
we go down
round
and round
the organ plays a vertiginous ditty

I get sick
I get sore
I get dizzy

When it stops I'm repaid for my pains
I get off then in the pub drown my ache
But just when I think I *could* be better
they take me to Holloway
and tell me I will *never* be better
because when I come out
they will have their money ready
and I will have my empty belly
and another mouth to feed
So the hand pulls the lever
and the merry-go-round
turns again

We go up
we go down
round
and round

I get dizzy
I get sick
I get sore

Mary Gale

Recidivist, 1910-11

17/09/10	prostitution – loitering	I had my own bed
01/10/10	drunken – riotous	I had clean clothes
19/10/10	ditto	I had regular meals
21/11/10	prostitution – loitering	I learned new skills
21/12/10	ditto	I had medical care
14/02/11	ditto	I was safe from harm
20/03/11	drunken – riotous	I had basic hygiene
19/04/11	ditto	I had a regular routine
29/04/11	ditto	I had companionship
16/05/11	ditto	I had a sense of purpose
21/06/11	prostitution – loitering	I had a roof over my head

The Baby Farmers

Sach, Amelia: Guilty of accessory to murder
– sentenced to death by hanging, February 3rd 1903 at 9am

Walters, Annie: Guilty of wilful murder
– sentenced to death by hanging, February 3rd 1903 at 9am

Amelia:

Ssh now, recline yourself dear.
Let me plump your pillows and offer
you the "accouchement" of which
the advert boasts: "before and during
… home comforts … baby can remain".

Annie:

Don't touch it – it's asleep.
Looks like a heap 'o rags
don't it? Rags that sigh
and cough and bark like dogs.

I am quite skilled: you can rest assured
when your time comes, you'll be in safe hands.
I'll dab your brow with my handkerchief,
watch you open like a bruised flower
and catch your screams in the net of my mind.

Ssh, it's sleepin', I told ye.
It needs a coupla drops
to get 'em off prop'ly
two little drops in its bottle.

There *there,* my dear. When it's over
I'll release you from your burden
– grown from the seed planted by a man
whose advances you drank like nectar
– and count your baby's fingers and toes.

Then they looks like little dolls:
all pearly white cheeks
and curled 'ands and feet
like daisy 'eads waitin' to open.

Tiny digits: pure, perfect bundle of love...
He'll be taken care of, don't you fret.
I have a lady of *class* most interested.
We'll dress him all up and she'll cherish him
so much she'll think her heart will split.

Dressed all fine-like in muslin
and lace. No – don't touch it!
You'll crease its gown
and then it won't be wanted.

For now, dear, *do* rest your mind,
finish the needlework you were inclined
to start for that lovely white gown
we'll bind him in when he's born.
That's it, dear – make the stitches tight.

Annie Selkin

Guilty of larceny – sentenced to 6 months with hard labour, 1904

It's my swift fingers, you see?
That's why they have me mostly
picking oakum or basket making.
Nimble and quick – how does the rhyme go?

She looked like she had enough so I took it
– it felt nice and thick in my hands.
I could almost hear it breathing;
still sealed, all fat and stamped.

We would've been all set
– me and the other half. A chance
at a new life overseas. Could've been happy,
maybe. He hasn't visited yet but he will.

Well these fingers won't be stealing again.
Mark my words. Look at them – red raw
and trembling. Yes, I'm done with that.
I'll tell him that too, when he comes.

*Stealing a post-letter containing a banker's draft for the payment
of £4 and a steamship ticket, the property of Fanny Bernstein.*

Queen Victoria

Her own words shaped into a suffragette

THIS

MAD,
WICKED
FOLLY

OF

"WOMEN'S
RIGHTS"

WITH
ALL
ITS

ATTENDANT
HORRORS

Lady Constance Lytton

Guilty of wilful damage – sentenced to 14 days, 1911

Dress a woman appropriately
and she can be
assigned to palace
or asylum
no matter what
is in her head and breast.
Accessorise her right for respect
or a life sentence as a doormat.
Have her speak a certain way
and she's honourable Lady
or fair game.
My alter-ego was poor Jane.
Fashioned from many boutiques
but her cause, heart, mind,
were the same.
She was punished more
for less of a crime.
Lady C broke windows,
yet gallant policemen escorted her away.
Jane was marched in an arm-lock.
Two wardresses stripped her,
then put her in the brown dress
of Third Division with hard labour
– an expectation of this class.
Lady C wore the neat green of First,
over specially requested underwear,
assisted by a brown-dressed inmate
who found shoes to suit her feet.
The staff were kind.
She got her vegetarian diet,
letter from her mother,
a private cell in the hospital,

medical attention by a doctor
who was proud to shake her hand.
Reprimanding was done, of course,
but it was done with a wink.
Jane's doctor straddled her knees
to feed her by force.
After the first time
he slapped her face
because, well, she was
restrained and he had these
emotions boiling and, well,
he could do it.
Eight attempts and he got
the tube length right
for her stomach.
She wore vomit-soaked clothes
till morning, lying
half-extinguished on the bed.
No one checked her heart
to feel its beat.
But Lady C's was diagnosed
with a weakness.
The perfect excuse
for special privileges
had I needed it.
Over this fluttering organ
I tattooed a V – for Votes.
Votes for all women.
And into the dressing
they smoothed over my wound,
soaked the blood
of poor Jane Warton.

Constance Lytton had previously spent one month in Holloway in February, 1909. As Jane Warton she was incarcerated at Walton Gaol, Liverpool.

Prison Cleaner

Third-division prisoner* at Holloway, 1909

Some people lead a charmed life;
stockingless feet, smooth and white,
told me she did. But she'd been naughty.

"Serves 'er right," they said.
"Little Miss La-di-da, sounding 'er
mouth off. Tryin' to pin 'er colours
to a place that don't feel no prick."

Sweet tar of carbolic.
My hands thick with suds.
Another layer of skin.

She's the thin-skinned type. Her veins
make river maps round her ankles.
Blue trickles of warmth I might
drown in if I was small enough.

I scrub with the stuff that was to be
my poison. Only I failed at that too.
Cleaned myself out.

Her type might laugh at this
in a different way. The Great Unwashed
and all that. It's not her fault. She was
brought up to expect more.

I expect nothing but the least. On my
knees where I belong. Absorb her sins
from the floor till it reaches a dull shine

that matches my skin.

A slow poisoning.
I take comfort, knowing
death will eventually come.

third-division prisoners cleaned the cells
of those in the first and second divisions.

Alice Hawkins

Guilty of disorderly conduct and resisting police – sentenced to 14 days, 1907

I'm a shoe-maker, but
you'll know me more for
riding a bike wearing bloomers.
Caused outrage in the papers.
Bloomin' ridiculous more like.
Stop the press when equal pay
makes front page and not our
unmentionables.

I'll give you outrageous!
How's this for headline news…
'King's Speech Neglects to Address
Women's Rights'. Never mind
bloomers on a bike. To be an
equal member of our own race,
why do we have to fight?

But we did. We marched on.
All sorts of us: bobbin-winders,
teachers, clay pipe finishers,
doctors, shirt-makers, power-loom
weavers. Carved our cavalry charge.
Us on foot, and them – horseback.
Not exactly a fair match for battle.
We got knocked, kicked, tripped,
jostled.

In this field we were not
'normal women', so rules could be
bent. One of them, she was lifted
from behind – the policeman's hands
clamped round her breasts –
then dropped face-down, skirts-up
and left.

Tell me why a woman who rides
a bike in bloomers
is so outrageous, and yet this is
not even worth a mention?

Black Maria

1912

Some think I'm named after a racehorse stunner,
(or a boarding housekeeper who "didn't take no shit.")
I like to think I'm a mix. A 'mother's heart', who always

has room for one more. I get all sorts scraping their feet
on my floor. Fixed in their lonely boxes. Upright coffins
with windows the size of hope. Some are full of rage

and rattle their irons in rhythms I've never heard before.
Many bellow their innocence over and over, bursting
with all the reasons they shouldn't be here. Some,

no more than skin on bone, stay silent, hearing their own
thin breath. All stare through the hope-sized window
realising they'd never before known what freedom

really looks like. When I'm full, (and that's often),
there's sometimes singing, but they change the words:
Glory, glory, Hallelujah! And the cause goes marching on.

(I don't need no convincing. I've always been strong).
Glory, glory, Hallelujah. And we all go marching on.
Glory, glory, Hallelujah. And *Black Maria* go marching on.

*The Black Maria was a horse drawn carriage which
transported criminals, secured within six individual
compartments, to Holloway Prison, and others.*

New Arrivals

Second and third division, 1908

We had to be silent, then
we waited in the reception cells.

We were called to the doctor, then
we had to strip off.

We were searched, then
our own clothes taken.

We gave our name, address,
age, work, religion, then

we had to bathe, while
they watched.

We had to get dressed
in green or brown

branded with arrows, then
walk to the main cells.

We had to wear a badge with
a number and letter, then

be known only by that
until we were set free.

Vera Wentworth

Given an extra day's sentence for writing 'Votes for Women' on cell wall, 1908

The Os are hardest
and three of them too, like singing mouths.
Two down, one to go
then 'men', and it's done.
Funny how they always
get the last word.
Oh, look at my nails!
Thin as paper and torn at the cuticles. I suffer
for my art!
I'll do the outline.
Someone must have seen.
I've had my eye on the 'eye' so to speak.
Sure I heard it twitch
from time to time.
They'll be reckoning up
a fitting punishment no doubt.
"Let 'er get it done then serve it up like skilly."
My comrade next door knows,
though to her
it must sound like rats.
There'll be no use trying to erase it, the whole wall
will have to come down!
One huge crumbling mess
with my etching riding
the wave of rubble like a ship refusing to capsize.
The unsinkable
Votes for Women!
Feel these letters
hacked out so beautifully
you could read them blind.
Now leave me to finish.
Carving is yet to be done.
But know I'll dream tonight of forfeits to come.

Smuggled Letters

Letter from Miss Alison Neilans *to Edith How-Martyn, written on toilet paper and smuggled out of Holloway Prison, 27th December 1909*

Extracts from a letter from Louisa Garrett Anderson *to her mother Elizabeth Garrett Anderson, undated, 1912*

Miss How-Martyn
    Dearest Mother
I have decided on the 'all'
    This is the most wonderful
and have commenced the secret fast
    experience I have ever had.
today Monday 27th. Of course
    Everyone is kind to us.
I may be found out.
    They have transformed the place.
Don't inquire before the 3rd, unless
    I am very well – indeed greatly rested.
you hear I am ill,
    I haven't had such a rest for years.
and don't worry – it's only
    I don't mind living on bread and butter
the same as we expected when I came here.
    and people allowed food give me scraps.
Don't tell Mother yet,
    It seems just a bit of good luck
but let Peter know.
    to come to Holloway.
Love to all of you
    I do hope you feel happy about us.
and my blessing on the cause.
    Very much love dearest,
AN
    Yrs LGA

Hospital Night Wardress

1909

You want to repay the favour
in one of the only ways possible
and I'm in need of love.

Your fingertips, cold and tentative
raise gooseflesh over my chest
as you gently rub.

The balm melts to liquid on my skin
and you watch, noting my reaction
to each touch.

I see your lips steadily twist
into a smile when there is no more
left to spread.

My flesh is raw as a prime cut
seasoned with camphor. Its scent
clings to our skin,

ready for the tasting. Later I will
smell its earthy tang while you
lather it off your hands.

You redo my dress, carefully, carefully,
so the oils don't stain. We resume our
roles. No one has seen.

Muriel Matters

Guilty of obstruction – sentenced to one month, 1908

First action*: convex body,
chest forward, arms by sides.

I wear chains like a chastity belt,
though I cannot rattle them yet.
The key slides down my dress;
I feel its stannic teeth nipping.
It wants me out too.

Second action: hands on hips,
legs spaced apart, feet flat on floor.

These restraints are my mechanism for freedom.
I am behind bars but I am not yet in prison.
Hear the men below?
Stretching their vocal chords
with such fervour they might perforate.
They hold the floor.
Then there is The Strangers' Gallery
– a whisper of a voice – then the cheap seats
– weaker still – then here, where I stand,
shadowed in bars behind the grille.
No place on the floor.
No *voice* at all.

* *inspired by the Delsarte method of acting*

(cont.)

*Third action: left hand cupped
behind ear, right hand shading eyes.*

Ladies are supposed to watch and listen.
And I *did*. I watched and listened
for my comrades in Strangers'
(not all men are bastards you know),
heard them holler 'votes for women!',
watched them release a flock of pamphlets
to sing of freedom over the floor,
heard the speaker calling 'order, order!',
the whole chamber in a flapping uproar,
while I locked myself in place.

*Fourth action: right hand under chin,
index finger resting on cheek.*

I imagine myself at Holloway,
changing into arrowed garb that chafes,
the wardress' face as the key falls
with a defiant 'plink' and she is forced
to check her jailor's set. The pair of us
locked in a tragicomic tableaux.

*Fifth action: both hands into fists,
arms stretched in front of body.*

They are coming for me now;
a pack of policemen all over six feet
(and I am the one causing the obstruction).
The cold key bites again. But it is safe.
Their only choice is to take down the grille.
Brute force dislodges it and for a moment
the window is as wide open
as a screaming mouth.

*Sixth action: arms outstretched to sides
of body, palms open and facing forwards.*

I taste the air of politics.
My opportunity, like the floodlit stage
when I first took to the boards, is here.
I move into the light.
I finally have the floor.
And there is so much

                         I want to say:

Kathleen Brown

Guilty of wilful damage – sentenced to 7 days solitary confinement, 1909

It was the nearest I'd get to returning from war.
Greeted in full splendour at Newcastle Central.
Carriages decked with loyalty, purity, hope.
A special reception at the Turk's Head.

Food.

I'd gone four days without. And I wasn't ready
for a feast. People said "Eat up. You've earned it.
Fill yer belly."

Finger sandwiches smiled. Iced fancies beckoned.
A well-meaning woman asked "What was it like, then?
Inside, like." I'd not yet thought of the answer.
I reckoned now I'm out, not that bad.

In there, alone and no food is a double punishment.
When hunger pangs grip your guts,
you bang the wall for answers.
You hear yourself reply in a voice that's not yours.

You sing through headaches and use exhaustion
to sleep off as much of the time as you can.
Dreams show you spreads like this. You wake up
licking your lips. After two days the pangs stop
and you are adrift for a while
before your body begins, bit by bit,
to eat itself.

With a smile, I said "Others had a far worse fate."
She said "That's good, pet – fill your plate."

Dr Francis Forward

Medical Officer at Holloway, 1913

My Quick and Easy Recipe for Forcible Feeding

Ingredients:
2 pints of milk
Beaten eggs
Vitamins as required
Other additives at discretion
of officer in charge

You will also need:
Length of India-rubber tubing
Lubricant
Funnel
Leather straps
6 personnel

Method: Restrain inmate using straps. Head must be in tilted-back
position. Lubricate tube for ease of insertion. Prise open inmate's
mouth. Insert length of tube until it reaches the stomach. Affix the
funnel to the top of the tube. Pour in the pre-mixed ingredients,
taking care not to induce a gag reflex. If inmate does vomit,
procedure can be repeated until the stomach is full. Note: if inmate
has an aversion to feeding by mouth, the nostrils can be used as an
alternative (tubing to be sized as appropriate).

Please note: This procedure will not endanger life
if the inmate refrains from mental excitement
before, during and after each feed.

Always follow instructions carefully
for amazing results each time!

Emily Wilding Davison

Guilty of arson – sentenced to 6 months, 1912

I knew the risks.
Each night they played
like a silent film before my eyes.

But I took them.

Melodrama is my mode.

Take a risk. Then if you pull it off,
you can smooth the deep creases
of the history books, penned
by heavy hands – men's hands.

What other woman could say
her abode was Parliament
(albeit a cupboard) on Census Day?

I was the *limelight lady*
each time they held me down
and threaded their tubes up
my nostrils. While a sour cocktail
of brandy and milk burned through me,
I saw myself not on the examining chair,
pinned by six men, but in a *mise-en-scène*
reclining on a chaise-longue,
hugged in silks and feathers,
my six suitors, arms outstretched,
each begging me to let *him* be the one
to light my cigarette.

This *dumbshow* played
forty-nine times.

Remember that
when your thought-clogged mind
debates whether
to mark a cross.

An Englishman

Letter written to Emily Wilding Davison whilst she was in a coma after being trampled by the king's horse at the Epsom Derby, 1913 – viewed differently

MISS DAVISON,
I AM GLAD
TO HEAR
YOU ARE IN
HOSPITAL. I HOPE
YOU SUFFER TORTURE
UNTIL YOU DIE.
I CONSIDER YOU ARE A PERSON
unWORTHY OF
EXISTENCE.
WHY DON'T
YOUR PEOPLE
FIND AN ASYLUM FOR
YOU?

Grace Marcon (a.k.a. Frieda Graham)

Guilty of damaging five paintings at the National Gallery
— sentenced to 6 months. In the exercise yard, 1914

Mr Photographer, I know you're there,
hiding in that black van, twitching
your fingers in the darkness. A hunter
waiting for the right moment to shoot.
After all, we are fair game. Led into place,
arm-in-arm with wardresses who pretend
friendship, until they are sure of the snap.
You want us there as it's your best shot.
Your long lens always hits that sweet spot.
And we smile, rest face or grimace on cue.
Mr P, do you whisper to us 'say cheese'?
Do you think of our esteem when you press
the shutter-release without our consent
and transform us into tawdry mugshots?
Perhaps seeing us in such baseness
turns you on? Maybe my hair undone
and all about my shoulders gets you
clicking. Or are you afraid, Mr Predator,
of what a woman in her natural state can do?
If only I could make you see beyond the
limits of your Model 2 tele-centric lens.
You are as much a prisoner as I. Enslaved
by the system that forces you to hide.
Groping in the shadows, rasping out 'yes'
each time you hit your mark. Can't you see
your debauchery? Compared to you I'm free.
So, go on Mr Hot Shot, take your likeness
but know I've seen the whites of your eyes.

Fred Pethick-Lawrence

Husband of Emmeline Pethick-Lawrence: she was
Guilty of conspiracy – sentenced to 9 months, 1912

I see you, dearest Em, lying
on that corpse bed in Holloway,
the walls closing in on your thinning body,
and I want to revisit that time when
I fell in love with a gloveless woman who
jumped prematurely off buses.
A woman whose name I took
as my own, to be as much
a part of her clan as she was mine.

Society calls me a hen-pecked husband
because it refuses to understand
my mind. Sexism makes my ordeal
in prison unnoteworthy, expected,
certainly not a martyrdom. Though
I suffer the same pain and exultation
I'm not supposed to
express either of them.

So I'll remain stoic
until my release
counting my fingers
and thumbs, taking comfort
in numbers and imagining,
dearest Em,
your sweet, darling face.

Fred received the same sentence as Emmeline and was imprisoned at Brixton.
He was force-fed twice a day for more than ten consecutive days.

Official Letter Template

Used in Holloway c.1912 when all correspondence was censored — blanks are reimagined

H M Prison *Holloway*
Dear *Mother*   19 *12*
I am now in this prison, and am in *Excellent* health.
If I behave well, I shall be allowed to write another letter about *How I have learned the errors of my ways* and to receive a reply, but no reply is allowed to this.   *Your loving daughter, Margaret*

H M Prison *In Hell*
Dear *God*   19 ?
I am now in this prison, and am in *dire* health.
If I behave well, I shall be allowed to write another letter about *nothing because I won't be behaving well* and to receive a reply, but no reply is allowed to this.   *Beelzebub*

H M Prison *Holloway*
Dear*est, loveliest Mum* 19 *12*
I am now in this prison, and am in *fair* health.
If I behave well, I shall be allowed to write another letter about
How there is not enough paper to say what I want to say to you.
I am so sorry if I have caused any hurt to you and the family.
I hope you will see that in the end it will have been worth it.
and to receive a reply, but no reply is allowed to this.
                    With all the love in my heart, Emily xxx

H M Prison **wherever**
Dear **whoever**   19 **whenever**
I am now in this prison, and am in **whatever** health.
If I behave well, I shall be allowed to write another letter about
whyever and to receive a reply, but no reply is allowed to this.
                    Anon

Katie Gliddon

Guilty of wilful damage – sentenced to two months, 1912

The rules said 'no unofficial paper'
but 'unobjectionable books' were allowed.
I challenge any smart woman to resist
a bit of Percy Bysshe, so yes,
Shelley's Poetical Works
were my writing materials
(and some pencils sewn into my coat collar).
Just enough to let my 'blithe Spirit' hover
somewhere beyond my body.

I pencil my colours in Shelley's margins;
the edges of his poems
shape my words and sketches,
both straight and ragged
in equal measure.
The Yang to my Yin.
Such a rarity this, written in confinement,
and funny that there is so much to say
when nothing happens at all.

Shelley is my rock. I feel his lines
snap like crackling between my teeth
then sigh as the taste seeps over my tongue.
I yell his sonnets through my window;
Ozymandias penetrates the courtyard gloom.
Then I fill his ample margins
with observations of all kinds of women,
all shapes, sizes, colours,
all exquisite in their own way.

I note the curve of a malnourished throat
and choose the shade for stippling
the skin tone. I note nicely pointed fingers,
imagining the sweet larceny they committed.
I note the pitch of a plaintive voice
chafing the night and paint clots
of vermillion over the sound.

Shelley's margins are my support, fulcrum,
bolster, stanchion, crutch, but,
whenever the pencil touches page,
I wonder what I'll do
when they are all full up.

Holloway Bomber

By the perimeter wall. Rear of Number 12,
Dalmeny Avenue. December 18th, 1913

Ssh! Come close. No, closer.
This is a delicate operation
for delicate hands; ones
that are meant for threading
needles and mopping brows.
Ha! We'll show them, eh? Sit
quietly there, by the wall but
be ready to spark it when I
give commands. Oh! I can
see the headlines now:
"Misguided woman tries
to bomb London Prison".
Their faces when they find
a lock of hair torn clean away
in the blast, waving from atop
the wall like a flag of surrender.
A tasty little enigma. How
misrepresented is our gender?
If they could only see my
delicate fingers now: filthy
with powder, reeking
of sulphur, shaking like mad
for what I'm about to do, or
undo, however you view it.

For the women over this wall
and beyond the bars; for
the women over the wall
behind me. Too long have
we been caged and gagged.
For the cause. Will you
whisper it too? Bless you.
I have my strand of hair
ready cut, and the ribbon.
Give them the tokens
they expect, to know this
was the work of a woman.
Now, ready my dear – to light?
Five, four, three, two, one...
...ignite!

Sylvia Pankhurst

Imprisoned eight times between February and July, 1913, under
Cat and Mouse Act (Temporary Discharge for Ill Health)

Cats toy with their prey
before releasing it, then
the game plays again
and again until it is dead.

Your Prison Act makes me
the mouse in this farce;
and you, you, play the cat.

Was I a mouse when I
stormed the courts with
banners of my own design?
Refused to pay the fine
and took prison as my
punishment, not because
'ladies prefer it' but for
the tactical publicity?

Do mice have tactics?

Was I a mouse when I
became the most feared
member of my family?
Sentenced so many
times, subjected to
torture so many times,
and remained strong
enough to tell my story?

My wee little mousie's tale.

Do mice fight for the
rights of their fellow
mouse? Do they want
equality for all breeds:
harvest, field, wood,
house? Would they
give up food, water,
sleep for the cause?

Mice are branded vermin;
dirty pests that multiply
and spread bacteria.
Do mice have an agenda
to improve conditions
for the entire murine race?

No.

They eat, sleep, breed,
and try to survive.
You, my friend,
are the mouse. Not I.

Mary Jane Clarke

Guilty of wilful damage – sentenced to one month, 1910

In here, frailness loses weight
thoughts chatter, voices evaporate.

On this pillow of thunder, I hear
the sea lapping against the pier

and I'm there, on the front
speaking my mind, taking the brunt

from rowdies and drunks, who see
me as some side-show rarity.

The sea is a fizzing tonic. It helps
the beach in its daily rebirth.

Yet it can't soften the edges
of an empty-shelled marriage.

We carry the names of our father,
then the names of our husbands,

like letters lodged in sticks of rock.
Right through the core.

My sister married a Pankhurst.
I married a Clarke.

But no matter our branding
we each beat our own destiny.

In here, I slowly dissolve. They
feed me up yet I waste away.

Like that strip of sand above the trash-line,
for me the tide will never come in.

He still holds the deeds to my life
and I have many foot casts over my skin.

Countess Constance Markievicz (née Gore-Booth)

Detained as an Irish Nationalist due to alleged 'German Plot', 1918

Darling, pour the wine.

We're celebrating my win
and from the Hard Nails Wing!
First woman elected.
My seat in the house so
unexpected.

But I'll never sit in it.

Not because I'm in here.
Lock me up and I'll only
want to fight for freedom.
Put me up on a stone bed
and my bones will strengthen.

No, because I can't stand
the blither. Stuff and nonsense!
And I can't sit comfortably
in the draughty institution
whose power takes freedom.

A drop more, darling. There.

No, I'll be the chairless MP.
Fated to roam the lands
with her gun in her britches.
Challenging the man
at any given chance.

(I will of course show my face
for appearances' sake
and check
my name's spelt right
on the cloakroom peg).

Now, pour a little more darling.

I have a speech to write.
And I must be properly fortified.

May McCririck

Gave birth alone in her cell, February 9th, 1919

I feel my waters burst
so I ring the bell.
At first
I don't think it's him coming
but he's been kicking like a mad 'un,
so I think he must be ready
even if I'm not. I see nothing
'cept a chink of moon on the floor.

No one comes
so I ring the bell again. I think
I hear scuffling down the corridor
but the sounds give over
to my own.
      Each wave I hear myself echo
back off the walls
like someone else
is going through it with me.

The pain is two fists in my back.
I joke to myself it's him
fighting his way out.
I can no longer reach the bell
so I pound the wall.
Another bell rings, then another,
way off in some other cell.

I smell my own blood.

By the time he comes
the moon has faded.

I finger my way round his shape
– perfectly formed. So warm.

I wait for his cry. Still
no one has come.

But the pain has gone.

I hold him to my breast
and wait for him to cry.

Ivy Cusden

Guilty of throwing sulphuric acid in a woman's face
— sentenced to 18 months, 1924

Look at you, my perfect little girl.
They've swaddled you up so tight,
it's maybe to stop you crying; like
you're wrapped in a massive hug.
You're a fresh sheet of linen, straight
from the market, not a stain in sight.
Pure white. No worries in the world,
save being well-fed, tidy and loved.
And rested, of course, but, Sleepy,
you're getting that now. No care
where you are, or that you had a
prison baptism. Your little eyes
are a-flutter. I wonder if you dream?

How could I have not wanted you?
I wasn't right. Not even twenty
and covered in marks. Thought love
had gifted me with a good man.
I had got *myself* pregnant, of course,
but he said he'd do the right thing,
and promised me a wedding ring.
This is your dadda, the upstanding
citizen. Turned out the right thing
for him was some other woman.

She bad-mouthed me all across town.
I'll save your ears from what she said
but it slurred me, blurred me. It hurt.
I got angry. With him, with her. But

mostly her. I had you in my belly
and knew it meant ruin. I wanted
to ruin what they had by ruining
her looks. I could see nothing else.
It wasn't till the flames had cooled
that I realised what I'd done. No
excuses. I was so sorry. Am sorry.
Will always be sorry. It's a burden
I'll have to carry, and so will she,
of course, till the end of our days.

I'm sorry I thought of giving you up.
But I don't suppose that matters
because they will take you anyway.

So many people fought for you
to be born outside these walls. So many
women to adopt you. So many men
to marry me. We made headline news.
You were famous from the inside!

Now I fear it will all fade
into a sentence of yesterdays.

But we have our time now, my
perfect little girl, so innocent
of the world. My baby behind bars.
Let me teach you what I know.

Ethel Smyth

Guilty of wilful damage – sentenced to 2 months, 1912

Having a jolly old hoot in Holloway
Playful ways to pass the time away
Join us in this grand old Holloway
Once you've seen it you'll want to stay

We make sweet songs by day and night
On toilet paper by gas light
'March of the Women' our exercise rhyme
Toothbrush as a baton helps mark time

Having a jolly old hoot in Holloway
Playful ways to pass the time away

We hang the yard white, purple, green,
Suffrage colours, fitness regime
Such camaraderie amongst women
In country tweed not lace and linen

Having a jolly old hoot in Holloway
Playful ways to pass the time away

We celebrate the cause with vintage wine
Ordered-in by our leader Emmeline
So relaxed, we access all the files
And plan our next strike across the tiles

Having a jolly old hoot in Holloway
Playful ways to pass the time away
Join us in this grand old Holloway
Once you've seen it you'll want to stay

Sir Henry Curtis-Bennett

Edith Thompson's leading counsel at trial, 1923

For shame, her imagination killed her.
Oh, I could have saved you, had you not
defied me and stood witness – but such
glamour! All dressed up like a Madam!
Her fancies secured her guilt. For shame.

Yes, her imagination killed her. "Laced
his dinners with glass", for shame.
Words of love were her ruin, not murder!
Oh, you extraordinary girl with your
desires. You were innocent! For shame.

No average woman or wife, she earned
more than some men, for shame. Oh you
obstinate, fanciful woman! And hanged
for her immorality, no more. Yes, for shame,
I'm certain, her imagination killed her.

I could have freed her.
I could have saved you, Edie,
I could have.

Edith Thompson

Guilty of lethal incitement and conspiracy to murder
— sentenced to death by hanging, January 9th 1923 at 9am

Once upon a time I used to dream
of fairy tales. I wanted to be
a Bluebeard damsel, not seeing
what I would suffer to be saved.

Happily ever after.

Percy was my Bluebeard. I loved
his power at first but it turned to bruises
that wouldn't whiten. "Only husbands
get divorces Mrs Thompson."

Happily ever after.

Freddie was my knight storming the castle.
I'd fed him with tales of wifely woe
so he'd slay the beast and catch me
fainting in his arms.

Happily ever after.

I didn't think he'd actually do it.
Foolish boy kept my letters. So here I am,
about to join Percy in Hell. Let's see
who burns blackest.

Happily ever after.

But, you see, they won't hang me.
They can't as I'm heavier now.
I'll get a stay. Yes, it's Freddie's.
And I was sick with it yesterday.

Happily
      ever
              after.
That's me.

John Ellis

Executioner of Edith Thompson, 1923

She had to be carried to the shed
but it wasn't like they said
that she "disintegrated as a human creature".

She was restrained and intoxicated
so it couldn't have been like they said
that she "screamed all the way".

She did bleed from her private parts
but it wasn't like they said
that her "insides fell out".

She was autopsied and declared
so it couldn't have been like they said
that "the drop was a coffin birth".

Mary Size

Appointed Deputy Governor, 1927

Oh, I am the Great Reformer
Nothing more than fair (but firm)

In my prison, women can dance
They are not punished further, for
Their punishment is being served
I incentivise with reward

In my prison, they get mirrors
And a means to buy makeup
They have to work for it, of course
A bit of friendly co-operation

In my prison, we are good friends
All inmates and staff, side by side
No more parading the freak show
Humanity and kindness rule

In my prison, all vacant cells
Become offices, workrooms, shops
Women are in paid employment
They have ambition, knowledge, scope

In my prison, broad skills are learnt
Child management to needlework
A way to maintain discipline
Without the inmates knowing it

Oh, I am the Great Reformer
Nothing more than fair (but firm)

Colonel Barker

*Née Lillias Irma Valerie Barker. Guilty of perjury and making a false
statement on a marriage certificate – sentenced to 9 months, 1929*

They were unprepared for a woman of my girth
so I'm waiting for a specially made set of rags
to cover my riddle of a body and make me regular.

Though on the outside I feel more like being Victor,
Valerie's still mostly me in body and mind.
She whispers me back from the edge sometimes.

As Valerie I did my duties as wife and mother;
gave up my maiden name and suffered
the bruises of matrimony in silence.

As Victor, handsome, charming, the world
was my conch shell. I visited Gentlemen's fitters
and took the liberty of Knighting myself.

Valerie always loved her sports and pranks
but they had to end with motherhood.
Victor could be a father *and* a player.

Yes, he was *that* charming. He taught boxing
and fencing to young fascists; advised them
on the perils of getting mixed up with women.

He became a Colonel and respected leader
of men. He bagged himself a bride who bought
his war-wound impotency yarn.

She considered their marriage to be quite
normal. He was attentive in other ways.
Quite the expert in fact.

He delivered convincing speeches to veterans,
jangling his (husband's) medals, recounting
his exertions in the Battle of Mons.

Like all good philanderers I was sent down
for bankruptcy, to Brixton, then Holloway,
when the doctor found my vulva.

They made me be Valerie for the trial:
wearing quivering fur boa to hide my face,
and stockings that felt like someone else's skin.

Recorder Wild said I was "an unprincipled,
mendacious, unscrupulous adventuress."
I said I'll take the adjectives but fuck the rest.

When I leave (the back way of course),
I will shed layers of Valerie onto the streets
and think about finding a new wife.

Harry Price

*Director of the National Psychical Research
commissioned to debunk Helen Duncan, 1933*

Imagine the scene: seventeen stone
of besmocked Scotswoman smashes
her husband in the face then dashes
into the street in a fit of hysterics.

We used science to uncover the woman's
fakery and determine where she was
concealing the "ectoplasm". Under
controlled conditions, we examined
her undergarments and external body,
then bound her to the armchair and
observed the "spirit voice" performance.

We took photographs of the
"materialisations" in twists and knots.

At one point we stopped her circulation.

But where was she hiding it?
We stiffened our fore-control and medically
explored every orifice of the woman's body.

Nothing.

Finally, we had our Eureka moment
– the last place to check: her stomach.

We had the woman. Her so-called
"ectoplasm", a rag of old cheese-cloth
she spewed from her mouth. Her so-called
"spirit guides" crudely fashioned
papier mâché dolls. Smoke, mirrors and
bare-faced brazen effrontery!

Due to my report, the woman became
more famous than ever. But in the end
convicted good and proper.

The last witch. Oh, yes,
I still like to congratulate myself.

Helen Duncan

Guilty of conspiracy under the Witchcraft Act of 1735
— sentenced to 9 months, 1944

Well, Harry paid me £50
so I had to put on a show.
I was always a bit that way, you know;
Aye, I often made my school friends cry
with my "dire predictions".

I earned my money in bleach
but people were so keen to believe
they could reach their bonnie ones
I shifted to séances.
It gave them some comfort
and put scran on my table.

What's the harm? Many more
men do this but are they harangued?
They are dismissed as charlatans, aye,
but not persecuted. Is it because
I am a woman or that I am fat
that bothers him most, I wonder?

Maybe he saw a glint of his own
demons in my eyes. For I do
have a gift, when I choose to use it.
I suffer for my art! Nosebleeds,
muscle ache from retching, sometimes
choking. It's a show, my wee 'uns

– you all know that now.
You wouldn't have been so foolish
as to investigate me. It's a job!
I have a manager and hired help
to put it on the road. So sue me!

When I was in gaol I read the Bible
to see if there was a God.
Some pages had been taken
for toilet paper. I wondered
if I could make ectoplasm.

Ruth Borchard

Refugee of Nazi oppression, detained for six weeks as an 'enemy alien', 1940

Alien: *noun*: a foreigner – *synonyms*:
non-native, immigrant, emigrant,
emigre, incomer, outsider, stranger,
newcomer, visitor.
I like visitor.
Yes. I could be your guest. I have
travelled here to escape.
The journey was long and tiring.
I won't be in your way forever
but while I am you could help.
It won't cost you much to do so.
Be the gentile, genial host.
Go on, invite me to tea if you dare.
I'm a newcomer, show me the ropes.

Get to know me
and I'm no longer a stranger.
Welcome me
and I'm no longer a foreigner.

Enemy: *noun*: actively opposed
or hostile to someone or something.
A thing that harms or weakens
something else.
I am the antonym.
Co-operative in all this chaos.
Calmly waiting in my cell.

Waiting for the real enemies
to destroy my clothes, to wave
a lit cigarette in my face, to say
I'm polluted for marrying a Jew.
For you to say we're all the same.
All suspects. Bloody foreigners.
Yet I have committed no crime,
caused no harm. Weakened no one.

Speak to me and you'll find out. Find
your own way of defining me
other than categorisation. A. B. C.

I may never see my daughter again.
Define my feelings for that if you can.

Prisoner whilst in Cell

Passing the time by remembering lines from
Shakespeare's sonnets, 1946

Shall I compare thee to a summer's day?
When in eternal lines to time thou growest.
In black ink my love may still shine bright.
In me thou see'st the glowing of such fire;
Who art as black as hell, as dark as night.
In me thou see'st the twilight of such day.
I all alone beweep my outcast state
Wishing me like to one more rich in hope.
Love alters not with his brief hours and weeks
But bears it out even to the edge of doom.
No longer mourn for me when I am dead;
From this vile world with vilest worms to dwell
For sweetest things turn sourest by their deeds;
Lilies that fester smell far worse than weeds.

The Mosleys

*Lady Diana Mosley (née Mitford) and Sir Oswald Mosley
imprisoned together under Defence Regulation 18B, 1941*

He loves dictators and I love *dictahtors*
I love autocrats and she loves *autocrahts*
Dictators, *dictahtors*, autocrats, *autocrahts*
Never call the whole thing off
No, darling, never ever call it all off

You see, we are meant to be: of one mind
and one body, when we melt in the sun
Golden martyrs with darker connections
How could we really have meant any harm?
Oh, we would never call the whole thing off

So, bring a bottle and darn well join us
in our delightfully private prison
Let the ordinary ones wait on us
How can we be a drain on the system?
Oh, we would never call the whole thing off

You see, she speaks Fuhrer and I speak *Fuhrer*
But I speak Hitler and he speaks *Hitler*
Fuhrer, *Fuhrer*, Hitler, *Hitler*
Never call the whole thing off
No, darling, never ever call it all off

*Inspired by 'Let's Call the Whole Thing Off'
lyrics by Ira and George Gershwin*

Prison Servant

One of two third-division prisoners assigned to the Mosleys'
accommodation in the grounds of Holloway Prison, 1942

I always listen
at the door, first.
It isn't always decent,
even if you knock.
Like they want us to see.

Eve and Adam
in various poses.
Not forbidden,
they got permission
to be as one.

All flesh, in their Garden of Eden
ripening
like wild strawberries.

Him bare-chested
with his nipples winking.
I'd be tempted
if I didn't know
who his friends were.

And anyway, there's her,
The 'lovely one'
made from
Hitler's missing rib,
its marrow hollowed out.

She flaunts her fruit
so beautifully
no one would know
there was a grub at the core.

While their bodies burn
he feeds her truffles.
She licks her lips
as their skin turns black.

I turn away
and leave them to it.
I'm not ready to see anything
like this just yet.

Diana Mitford

Detained under regulation 18B, 1940

They said only a weekend.
Almost makes a holiday of it.
"Fairy Castle Fantasy Getaway".
Ideal if your dream escape is
dark, rank, confined spaces.
"Come and spend a long weekend
with us – a restful retreat for new
mothers – all-inclusive package deal."
Bed down in a broom cupboard for
four hours straight. "So peaceful.
The perfect break away from it all."

Well the weekend is long over
and cupboard has turned to cell.
Eleven weeks and weaned overnight,
my baby mourns his mother's milk.
It permeates my clothes like shame.
The ache is worse after lights out.
All that blackness and nothing to
focus an agile mind upon, except
the arid sound of women sobbing.
I convince myself it is him
unleashing his hunger cry.

I want to bind my breasts
with salts and bandages
so they can heal. Cage them
for their own benefit, like
a lunatic in a straightjacket.
I will collect all the milk I can
but have to accept in defeat
that in here I may dry up.
Never before have I needed
a human being so much, and
never before felt so redundant.

Barbara Roads

Guilty of conscientious objection
– sentenced to one month, 1943

You ask me why I choose
to do this, choose
to refuse my war duties
by not signing up with the warden,
choose to challenge the system,
choose to be pregnant in prison?

You think it's easy enough
to sign up for something
you don't believe in
just because it's the done thing.
Scratch you name on
someone else's skin.

Do these women choose
to be pregnant in prison?
Choose to eat for two
on extra milk and bread?
Choose solitary confinement
until the baby's due
because the hospital's full?
Choose a cell bell that's dull
or no one's there to hear it,
or no one who hears it cares
enough, and no one comes?
Choose to give birth alone?
Does any woman choose that?
Can't you see she was at the
crippled ends of her wits?

I choose to refuse because
they asked me to do it.
And you can only refuse
what you are asked to do.
Ask me to join the army
and I'll refuse that too.

Prison is a choice for me.
I can handle a month and make
my point. In utero, my baby
won't know anything. No harm
done. Being behind bars
is a chance for freedom.
Choosing to refuse
wins choice. Choice
for a future
where you
can say no and not
be sent to prison.

Jean Rhys

Guilty of assaulting a neighbour
— sentenced to one week on remand, 1949

"You'll never learn to be like other
people," said Mother. Another voice
that wanted to be written down.
I hear them all the time, and my pen
cannot keep up. I don't like scrawl.
The Creole way is slow and careful.
She was right; I never did learn.
But why are we taught to be

the same as others? Why are we
not taught that difference is good?
I could have mastered this and
passed with flying colours; been
better equipped for ridicule; seen
'white cockroach' as something
rare, not a weapon for self-loathing.
"You shut me in," says Selina, my

character. My own careful creation.
My pen tries to keep up. Less
speed, more haste. "But," she says,
"You shut out all those other damn
devils. They can't reach me now."
This castle keeps her safe, from
men who can't decide whether to
protect or exploit. From women

who are neither winners or losers.
From neighbours who don't show
love, and force her to crack. From
paradoxes. Selina's skin is darker
than mine. They hated her for it.
Called her dirty. Flung her clothes
on the floor. We dance the same;
moves they don't know, can't follow.

It scares them and they hate us
more for it. In here we are safe.
Mother was both wrong and right.
Another paradox. I did never learn
to be like others but someone else
is a lot like me. The magistrate
kept ordering her "silent" but
her voice keeps me awake at night.

Prisoner whilst in Punishment Cell

Solitary confinement, 1948

When
I hear that
rattle, rattle, rattle
of keys I make up games
to stop the noise. What is a rattle
when you really think about it?
A clank, clink, clunk, bang or clang?
Is it on the door or through the walls?
Perhaps it can be many things at once.
It's jingle jangle coins in your pocket.
A snake's tail tease or someone's cage.
It's a rapid recitation of facts like bullets,
the ones fired at those poor Doomed Youth.
Or prattle, babble, gabble when you're
going on and on and on and on and on,
like me with this load of old twaddle.
It wakes you with a jolt, jounce, judder.
It fazes, flusters, ruffles your feathers,
throws you off balance, puts you off
your stroke. Listen really really
carefully and it's that sound
coming from my
throat.

Styllou Christofi

*Guilty of murder – sentenced to death by hanging
at 9am on December 15th, 1954*

(Translated from the Greek)

They said I murdered my daughter-in-law.
Set her body on fire.
I feared for my grandchildren
but I did not kill her.
I gave my evidence in Greek.
The prosecutor called me "stupid woman
of the illiterate peasant type".
The doctor declared me insane.
My son heard me repeat my innocence,
in English and Greek. I said
that three men committed the crime.
My hometown vouched for my character.
I did not plead insanity.
I was denied the chance to speak in court.
My condition was not noted in prison.
My son refused to see me.
The Governor misspelled my name.
I asked the Greek church lady
to bring me biscuits. I waited.
I asked for a cross to be hung
in the execution chamber.
The hangman noted my tears.
The press had no interest in
a grey-haired mad old Greek woman.
Her wedding ring was in my jewellery box.

Theresa Mackenzie

Guilty of stealing her employer's jewels
– sentenced to 3 years, 1948

Four walls is all I need, honey.
And space to move in between.
And boy do I move. Sometimes
I play; they allow me my mandolin.
My agent insisted I practise my art.
Because when I get out I'll be a star.
I shake my hips like Josephine.
Try it with me, sugar…

…Hand on hips.
A side thrust to each corner.
Clockwise. Anti-clockwise.
Then forward thrust to each wall,
like making the sign of the cross.
Shimmy, shimmy, shimmy, honey.
Think of cracking coconuts.
Backward thrust to the window,
then the door. Try to time it for
when the officer unlocks it.
Hold this position.
Wait for the reaction.
Then turn, wink, smile, straighten.
Musical interlude. Then get ready
to go again…

I'm something even in prison.
Imagination gives me
a cream satin slip, split
to the thigh, headdress and fans
of black swan feathers. Fish net
stockings with the seams up
the back, the ones you can trace
with your fingers. And a string
of jewels, not heavy as shackles, but
light and precious as a silver lining.

Now I have to practise.
Look for my name when I get out.
I'm going to be a star
just like Josephine Baker.
Did you hear that, sugar?

Borstal Girl

Aged 16 (has been on probation since she was 9 years old)
– sentenced to 3 years Borstal detention, 1949

Take a girl like me – call me
a runaway, unruly, out of control,
no respect for institutions,
stupid, lazy
shallow, liar, retarded, anxious, silly
sly, selfish, irresponsible,
attention-seeking.
Bewildered.
Mentally disturbed.
Fallen.

Call me that if it's easier for you.
Hysteric. Weak.
Easier for you, isn't it?
Easier than dealing with me.
Me.
The broken but still breathing
thing at your feet.

Give me a criminal record
because a man touched me
before my time. Like I am the one
who's committed a crime.

No respect for institutions. I hate
institutions. Wouldn't you
hate institutions if you were me?
Why am I blamed for bad things
done to me? Too quickly.

Bloody right, too quickly. Go find
him and lock *him* in irons. Hose
him down with freezing water, till
he crumples in a soggy mess .
and takes the blame for what he's
done, no matter whether he did it or not.
Do *him* for insubordination
and take *his* food and water.

That wouldn't work for you, would it?
No, I'm here, and I look
like trouble so I must be trouble.
I *am* trouble.
And you've made me worse trouble.
Now you'll have to punish me.
A naughty girl. A very poor type.
Deal with me.

Take a girl like me – call me
a runaway, unruly, out of control,
no respect for institutions,
stupid, lazy
shallow, liar, retarded, anxious, silly
sly, selfish, irresponsible,
attention-seeking.
Bewildered.
Mentally disturbed.
Fallen.

Mollie

Guilty of manslaughter – sentenced to 7 years
In the hospital, 1950

There was a young woman called Mollie
Who used to be so wild and jolly

Would you like to see
the photograph?
They're keeping an eye on me
here, in case I lose it again.

At sixteen she married
And from then never tarried
From filling her belly with dollies

See the photograph?
That's Jack – he would have turned five
this year, and little Chrissy, see?
would have turned three, today actually.

Three popped out before she turned twenty
She thought that it had to be plenty

It's like a shroud came down
after the first and it never lifted.
He left because I couldn't manage
and went to find a woman who could.

But her man didn't stay
And two wasted away
So now she's in here to repent

My third's still alive,
and I'm terrified
they'll take her away.
I'm unfit you see.

There was a young woman called Mollie
Who used to be so wild and jolly

I have more photographs…
Would you like to see them?
See there? That's Jack
He would've turned five this year.

Executioner Pierrepoint

Cap   Noose   Pin   Lever   Drop

Cap... It was in part a calling, my craft.
I was put on Earth to do it. My father
told me, aged eleven, that one day
I'd become the 'Official Executioner'.
My mission, my one-man expedition
passed down from him to me. I thought
it just the job for me: travel, adventure,
death, romance. Like poor Uncle Johnny
whistling his way to the barbed wire fence.
Even my teacher smiled when I replied
to that old question: "What do you want
to be when you grow up?" Well, it was
either that or work with horses.

Noose... Father told me some stories:
his training days getting a nose for the craft.
Tightening the noose on sandbag dummies.
Calculating and recalculating the drop,
their crudely stitched faces grinning all
the way down (someone's idea of a joke).

Pin ... He kept a diary of executions: a thick
black tome – The Grim Reaper of books, like
a family Bible. He entered each detail piously:
name, age, height, weight, condition of neck.
It was a science to him but he remembered
them all, knowing it was he who always
looked them last in the eyes.

Lever … Each journey to the scaffold was
singular: the painful comedy of a man
complaining about the tightness of the rope.
The pathos of another who was allowed
to smoke, his cigarette still held between
his lips when they cut him down.

Drop … Now I carry the tools of this trade:
rope, rule, wire, shackle, measure, pliers, cap.
My calf-leather wrist-strap, reserved for
special cases, torn eyehole-to-eyehole by
the rage of a German spy.

Cap   Noose   Pin   Lever   Drop
There's a rhythm to this business. You have
to get it right to avoid any unnecessary
stress. It's no different for a woman, except,
for decency we adjust the leg-strap. They
are always braver than men. But I treated
them all the same. Even The Beautiful Beast:
"Schnell, schnell… Make it quick!"
I always did. Knot under left jaw for a clean
break. Swift end. Respect in death.

Ellis went without a last word, despite what
the papers said. Let them print their tangled
lies. The last woman I will hang. *Cap… Noose…
Pin…* My ambition's fading. Executions solve
nothing. *Lever… Drop…* nothing.

Did I tell you she never spoke a word?

*Albert Pierrepoint hanged 433 men and 17 women in his career,
including Ruth Ellis, executed at Holloway Prison on 13ʰ July 1955.
He resigned his post on 23ʳᵈ February 1956.*

Anne Pierrepoint (née Fletcher)

Wife of Albert Pierrepoint, at home, 1945

His next letter rests peacefully
on the mantelpiece, officially
stamped and sealed in black
like the news poised inside.

He's only just told me his secret
but really I rumbled him long ago.
I unearthed his thick black ledger
with all those names and particulars

scribed ever-so-carefully in straight
and regular lines. I pretended it was
a book of condolences at first
but the hard facts breathed out.

After those times away he always
comes home with a hunger and I
always have his favourite ready.
Then he sleeps like a full tankard.

His money tin's beginning to swell
and I have plans for our future. We
will invest in a public house and I'll
be landlady, keeping things steady

while he does his duty. Better
than delivering groceries, surely.
He's the quickest in the country
– did he tell you that? Hanged

a man in seven seconds. He takes
such pride in doing a decent job.
But it's brass tacks with us only.
Down to me mostly. If I know so much

that I can sketch pictures of them
in my mind, I am surely unlikely
to ever get it back. It's best that way.
No, I never, never ask any questions.

Hush now, I hear his key in the lock.
Don't let on that you know anything.
He hates people knowing what he does.
I'll just put that letter back where it was.

Juror

At the trial of Ruth Ellis, Court 1, Old Bailey, 1955

Fellow Gentlemen of the Jury,
we need a verdict
and she clearly did it.
Therefore, do we find her
guilty of murder?
Is   she   guilty?

Is she guilty
of being a nightclub hostess,
an adulteress,
three men on the go at once,
divorced, bottle-blonde,
promiscuous.

Is she guilty
of being emotionless,
calculated and calm,
an assertive killer, commanding
"Now call the police".
For saying, "I intended to kill him".

Is she guilty
of being jealous and rejected,
hurt and humiliated.
For choosing abusive men
and forgiving so easily.
For *bruising* so easily.

Is she guilty
of being a bad mother,
pregnant out of wedlock.
Miscarrying because
she was thumped in the tummy
by a man who said he loved her.

Is she guilty
of being young and attractive:
a tart, a temptress, a whore.
Because her high heels make
a clicking sound when
she walks across the floor.

Fellow Gentlemen of the Jury,
we need a verdict
and she clearly did it.
Therefore, do we find her
guilty of murder?
Is   she   guilty?

Officer Evelyn Galilee

In charge of Ruth Ellis whilst in condemned cell, 1955

You could say
   that this cell was moulded
      from plastic
or had the stuff poured in.

I remember that morning
   holding tight
      to the water pipes
to see if they would snap.

They poured her into here
   and she set
      like a doll
never to be broken again.

You could almost see
   the tiny fractures
      in her skin
glued from the last breaking.

She wasn't the brassy tart
   they all said she'd be.
      Her damage
had gradually let in the light.

Bright as the naked bulb
   that burned
      over her head
for three weeks straight,

but naïve as a young girl
   sitting so tiny
      at her table
making dolls of her own.

Or holding the open compact
     to her face
          making herself up
to the tune of La Vie en Rose.

In her small voice
     she kept asking
          about the large screen
and what it was hiding.

They gave her plastic cutlery
     for fear of what she'd do
          with metal.
But she was so composed.

Even when that morning came
     and I helped her dress,
          watched her fingers
close the compact one last time,

she was anything but
     the hysterical moll
          they'd painted her as.
No, she was cool as porcelain.

I can still see her face
     moulded into a thin smile,
          mouthing 'thank you' at me
when they took her through.

The pipes burned
     – metal after all.
          I held on
for as long as I could

then I extinguished the bulb.

Ruth Ellis

Guilty of murder – sentenced to death by hanging,
July 13th 1955 at 9am

The noose was poised
like a priest between us.

Do you take this woman?

He looked me right
in the eyes, his breath spiked
with his last cigar, taking me

back to the club. The smell I lived.
And endured when they wanted
more than they could afford.

I now pronounce you man and wife.

They'd done me up nice.
Got me my lipstick and bleach.
I was looking like a prize.

I may have smiled. I wanted to,
I remember. Thought he needed
a bit of kindness. He had such

a serious look about him.
A frown you could slide down
and land in his eyes.

You may now kiss the bride.

I smelled an earthy scent
on his fingers as he placed
the hood over my head.

Then my story became
a blank page. I saw colours
and shapes and a smiling face.

I pictured him later, cutting me
down, gently holding me,
undressing me, laying me out.

Voices through the Walls

going on and on and on and on and on

                   it must have been a mistake

                         it was done with a wink

          listen really really carefully

      rats scratching in the walls

blue trickles of warmth

      pass the time away

I have a speech to write

         I will never be better

               catch me if you can

                   I fill his ample margins

           I could almost hear it breathing

      compared to you I'm free

will always be sorry

      watch over me

evidence acquired

      now you'll have to punish me

         I've seen the whites of your eyes

                   rattle, rattle, rattle

                its warm belly growls

      is it on the door or through the walls

going on and on and on and on and on

Camden Castle

A colloquial name for Holloway Prison

My designer was "more practical than artistic".
A House of Corrections, I am the schoolmistress
of buildings. Each of my cold stones was laid
to the rhythm of the clock not the heart.
      I'm strong, sturdy, stable, most certainly
      from the outside; a perfect gothic castle
      with battlements, crenellations, machicolations
      the lot! I bet if you could reach
my buttresses, you'd want a feel.
Inside I am soft. If you cut me
down the middle and took a slice
it would be Baked Alaska.
      I'm full of melting Ice Maidens
      all praying for their times to come.
      But however they leave me, they leave me cold.
      I'm built on land intended for Cholera graves.
Rotten irony. Now I'm here, nothing's changed.
They create the disease then think they have the cure.
Come and spend some time in me and learn wrong
from right. Repent your sins. What a joke!
      On my foundation stone is etched:
      MAY GOD PRESERVE THE CITY OF LONDON
      AND MAKE THIS PLACE A TERROR TO EVIL-DOERS.
      Like I said, my designer was "more practical than artistic".

Henry Mayhew

In his own words from an account of a prisoner, 1862 – reshaped

A
young
man,
about
nineteen
years of age,
of a pale thin
countenance,
with a vacant eye,
evidently of
imbecile
mind,
was led
into the
reception
warder's
office.

Reception Warder

In his own words, 1862 – re-presented

Have   you   any   friends
to   receive   you   when
you   leave   the   prison?
Were   were   were   you
ever   in   p p prison   before?
W ww   w   what   was   it
which   innnduced   you   to to
commmmit   this   fel felony?
Have   you   le   le   le   learned
any   business   any   business?
Are   you   g g gg going t t t
to   keeeeeeeeeeeep   out
of   b b b b bad   commmmpany
in in in   the   f f f fff future???

Young Man, about Nineteen Years of Age

1862

When I answered him, all
I could hear were the words
dead   head   shed   bed.
My voice never sounds like
mine, you see. I always feel like
I'm hearing myself from over
the river, calling to myself
through the morning fug.
Only certain words get through:
dead   head   shed   bed.
Do I even say these words
or are they said differently
to suit his ears? My father is
dead. I'm not right in the
head. I often sleep in the
shed for I rarely have a *bed.*
I sound like one of those boys
in the rhymes. The naughty ones
who get punished in the end.
I suppose these words must
be mine because they sound like
me: the Little Boy Lost, on the
wrong side of the river.

Two Prisoners

On their release from Holloway, standing outside the prison gates, c.1880

Prisoner 1: I am leaving this place a changed woman. You?

Prisoner 2: I don't see 'ow I can e'er change. Why?

Prisoner 1: I have a shilling in my pocket. You?

Prisoner 2: My pockets is turned out. Why?

Prisoner 1: They gave me new shoes for my walk home. You?

Prisoner 2: I couldn't tell 'em I need shoes. Why?

Prisoner 1: Father will be waiting for me in the city. You?

Prisoner 2: No-one is waitin' for me there. Why?

Prisoner 1: I learned a trade in here: basket-weaving.
It will get me somewhere. You?

Prisoner 2: I couldn't do lessons.
No point. Why?

Prisoner 1: My physical health is good. I am fit to work. You?

Prisoner 2: My weak chest only got worse in there. Why?

Prisoner 1: From now on I will stay away from bad company. You?

Prisoner 2: Bad company's likely to seek me out. Why?

Prisoner 1: I feel nervous and excited. You?

Prisoner 2: I'm full of dread. Why?

Prisoner 1: I will celebrate my release tonight.
Penance done, straight and narrow. You?

Prisoner 2: I'll be drownin' me sorrows
with someone else's money. Why?

Prisoner 1: No matter. And so it begins; my walk
to the city and a fresh start. A free
woman with fire in her heart.

Prisoner 2: I can't walk that far, and the pub's
o'er the road. Its warm belly growls.
My story ends 'ere. Why? No matter.

Sir Robert Carden

Former Lord Mayor of London (1857-8) and magistrate, 1880

Smoke, mirrors, open the trap door
It doesn't matter what you've done
If you're guilty, your time has come
Hell always has room for one more

You may be a loiterer
Waiting for a chance
To help your poor mother
Who's danced her last dance

Or a beggar disgraced
Nearly ninety years old
Widowed and denied a place
So lonely, hungry and cold

Smoke, mirrors, open the trap door
It doesn't matter what you've done
If you're guilty, your time has come
Hell always has room for one more

You may be a deserter
Served your regiment for years
Witnessed all kinds of horrors
And bullied by your peers

Or a rogue incorrigible
Getting into scrapes
To feel much less horrible
Than that night you escaped

Smoke, mirrors, open the trap door
It doesn't matter what you've done
If you're guilty, your time has come
Hell always has room for one more

You may be a drunkard
As motherhood was so brief
Gazing into the tankard
To dull the pain of grief

Or a prostitute so poor
Tainted at a tender age
There just wasn't a cure
For his violence and rage

Smoke, mirrors, open the trap door
It doesn't matter what you've done
If you're guilty, your time has come
Hell always has room for one more

References

Epigraphs

Louisa Garrett Anderson to her mother Elizabeth Garrett Anderson from Holloway Prison (1912) Women's Library Archive letters (WL: 7LGA/1/2/7)

Margaret Atwood (1998) *In Search of Alias Grace: On Writing Canadian Historical Fiction*, The American Historical Review

Elizabeth Neilson (1955) *Ruth Ellis: 10 Days to Go. Mother Cries "Why Torture Her?"* Sunday Dispatch, 3 July

By Poem

Emma Mary Bird: Register of Prisoners Committed for Want of Sureties at City New Prison Holloway (LMA: CLA/003/PR/06/001)

The Order of the Administration of the Lord's Supper or Holy Communion: Printed Book of Communion and Other Services (LMA: CLA/003/CP/05/002)

Major Arthur Griffiths (1902): 'In Holloway Prison' article for Living London Volume 1 edited by George Sims, Cassell & Co. Ltd., 1902

Mary Gale: Record of Convictions 1910-1914 (LMA: CLA/003/PR/01/001)

Annie Selkin: Printed Calendar of Prisoners 1903-1904 (LMA: CLA/003/PR/05/001)

Queen Victoria: Her letter to Sir Theodore Martin in 1870

Smuggled Letters: Mrs Alison Neilans to Edith How-Martyn 1909 (WL: 9/20/183) and 8 Letters of Louisa Garrett Anderson to her mother Elizabeth Garrett Anderson smuggled out of Holloway Prison 1912 (WL: 7LGA/1/2/4)

Printed with permission from The Women's Library LSE and Dr Jennian Geddes, acting on behalf of the Garrett Anderson family.

Katie Gliddon: Prison Diary 1 – Katie Gliddon 1912 (WL: 7KGG/1/1)

May McCririck: Dr Rachel Bennett 'Identifying and Advocating for Women's Health: The Duchess of Bedford's 1919 Committee of Enquiry into Medical Care in Holloway Prison'

The National Archives, Holloway Prison: Duchess of Bedford Enquiry (PCOM: 7/40/32-33)

Barbara Roads: 'Some Account of Life in Holloway Prison for Women', published in 1943 by the Prison Medical Reform Council

Prisoner Whilst in Cell: Lines from Shakespeare's sonnets, Lines 1-2: Sonnet 18, line 3: Sonnet 65, line 4: Sonnet 73, line 5: Sonnet 147, line 6: Sonnet 73, lines 7-8: Sonnet 29, lines 9-10: Sonnet 116, lines 11-12: Sonnet 71, lines 13-14: Sonnet 94

An Englishman: Hate mail to Emily Wilding Davison from An Englishman June 1913 (WL: 7EWD/A/7/5)

WL – Women's Library

LMA – London Metropolitan Archives

Select Bibliography

Fran Abrams, *Freedom's Cause: The Lives of the Suffragettes*, (Profile Books, 2003)

Alfred Aylmer, 'Detective Day at Holloway' from *The Windsor Magazine* (Ward, Lock & Co., 1897)

John Camp, *Holloway Prison: The Place and the People*, (David and Charles, 1974)

Rose Collis, *Colonel Barker's Monstrous Regiment: A Tale of Female Husbandry* (Virago, 2001)

Rupert Croft-Cooke, *Bosie – The Story of Lord Alfred Douglas* (W H Allen, 1963)

Caitlin Davies, *Bad Girls: A History of Rebels and Renegades*, (John Murray, 2018)

Joan Henry, *Who Lie In Gaol* (Victor Gollancz Ltd., 1954)

Leslie Howsam, *Atlantis, Volumes 15-16 'Sound-Minded Women": Eliza Orme and the Study and Practice of Law in Late-Victorian England'* (Institute for the Study of Women: University of Minnesota, 1989)

Annie Kenney, *Memories of a Militant* (Edward Arnold, 1924)

Carol Ann Lee, *A Fine Day for a Hanging: The Ruth Ellis Story* (Mainstream, 2012)

G. Lewis, *Regulations for the Government of the City Prison at Holloway* (Court of Alderman, 1860)

Constance Lytton, *Prisons and Prisoners: The Stirring Testimony of a Suffragette* (Heinemann, 1914)

J. Marlow (Ed.) *Votes for Women: The Virago Book of Suffragettes* (Virago, 2000)

Henry Mayhew and John Binny, *The Criminal Prisons of London and Scenes of Prison Life* (Griffin, Bohn, and Company, 1862)

Albert Pierrepoint, *Executioner Pierrepoint* (Eric Dobby Publishing, 1974)

Harry Price, *Leaves from a Psychist's Case-Book*, (Victor Gollancz, 1933 (chapter XI))

June Purvis, *The Prison Experiences of the Suffragettes in Edwardian Britain* (Women's History Review, 1995)

R.F. Quinton, *Crime and Criminals 1876-1910* (Longmans, Green & Co. 1910)

Anne Schwan, *Convict Voices: Women, Class, and Writing About Prison in Nineteenth-Century England* (University of New Hampshire Press, 2014)

René J.A. Weis, *Criminal Justice: The True Story of Edith Thompson* (Penguin Books, 1988)

'*Rare Birds* is a thought-provoking collection that gives voice to a broad range of the people who lived and worked in Holloway during its 164-year history, and offers a fresh and engaging way of looking behind the prison's turreted walls. In addressing the themes of motherhood, health, and reform, the poems speak in a creative way to the historical experiences of women in prison.'

DR RACHEL BENNETT (Research Fellow for the Wellcome Trust Senior Investigator Award 'Prisoners, Medical Care and Entitlement to Health in England and Ireland, 1850–2000')

'A powerful and emotive collection reflecting how little incarceration, and the impact it has on the lives of those affected, has changed through the decades. There are clear lessons to be learned from the eloquent and passionate accounts of lived experience, yet the Criminal Justice System still has a long way to go in truly hearing those voices. It struck me that the echoes of the past are the voice of now – we must listen and act, to improve the future for those requiring rehabilitation and resettlement.'

EMMA FALK (Operational Manager, Ripon House Approved Premise – rehabilitation of offenders)